The Romans won the first round, but storms stopped Caesar's back-up troops reaching him. The Celts saw that the Romans were in a dodgy position and attacked again. The Romans won the second round too. But Caesar knew it was only a matter of time before the Celts beat him.

The following year Caesar came back with 27,000 soldiers. This time, Cassivellaunus, an important Celtic chief, struck a deal with the Romans. Caesar left Britain, taking hostages and valuable information about Britain. Nearly 100 years passed before the Romans invaded again.

The Roman army fought the Celts on the beach near Deal, Kent.

The Romans conquer

In AD 43, the Roman Emperor Claudius decided to invade Britain big time! His army of about 40,000 soldiers landed at Richborough in Kent.

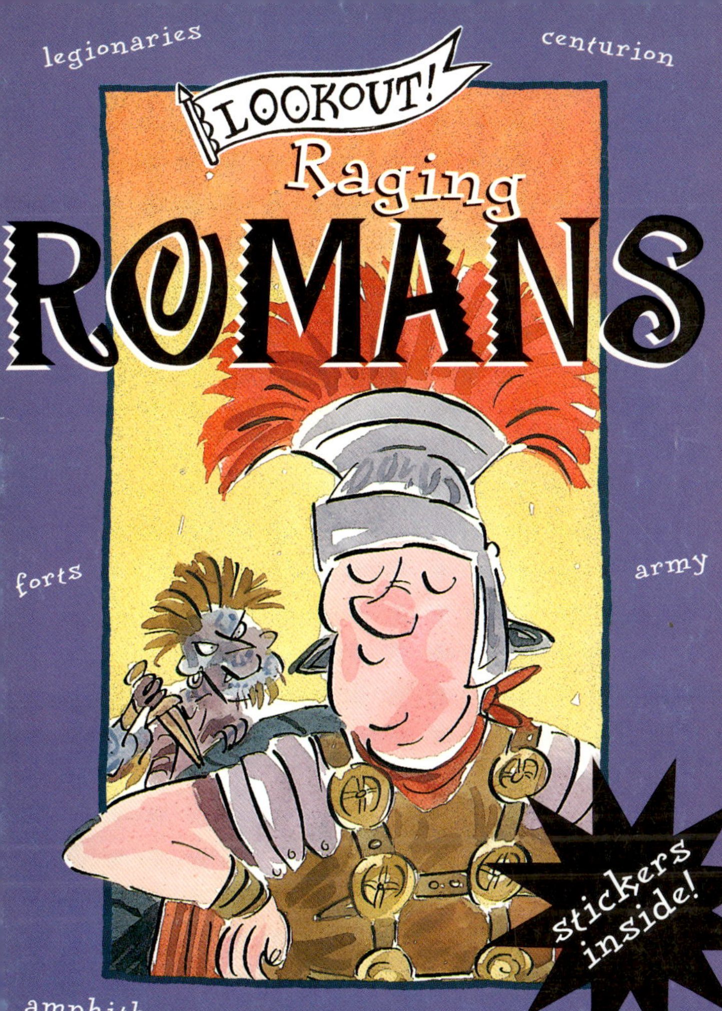
legionaries
centurion
LOOKOUT!
Raging
ROMANS
forts
army
stickers inside!
amphitheatres
auxiliaries

The Romans invade!

In 55 BC, Julius Caesar invaded
Britain with a small army of
soldiers. The Roman army landed on
the Kent coast
and fought
against the Celts.

Caesar had warned the Celts he was
planning to invade. He hoped they
would surrender without a fight. But
thousands of Celtic warriors were
waiting for him on the beach in full
battle cry.

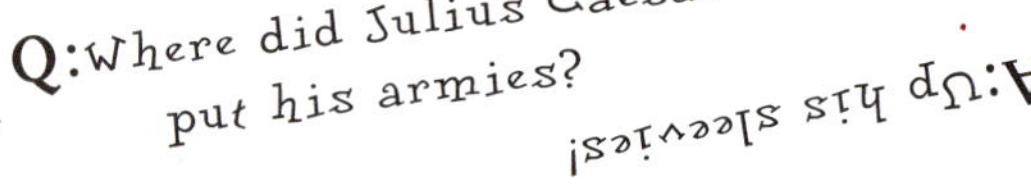

Q: Where did Julius Caesar put his armies?

A: Up his sleevies!

The Romans marched towards Colchester, an important Celtic religious centre. They fought many bloody battles on their way. At Colchester, 11 Celtic chiefs surrendered. The Romans soon controlled the south of Britain.

In the next few years, a town grew up around a bridge the Romans had built across the River Thames. It became a place where important roads met and where ships could deliver goods. The Romans named the town Londinium. Soon, it became the capital of Roman Britain.

The arrow marks the spot where the Romans built a bridge across the River Thames.

Lookout!

Look out for Roman weapons in museums. Find out what you score on page 14.

4

Marching onwards

With the south under Roman rule, the army marched to Wales and Scotland. Soon it controlled Wales, and as far west as Exeter. Scotland was more difficult.

As the Romans marched, they built bridges and straight roads so soldiers could travel long distances at great speed. Every road was measured in miles and marked with milestones. Rest-houses were built along many routes for use by Roman officers, inspectors and messengers.

The Romans built forts as bases for the army. Forts were always built to the same pattern with stables, barracks, offices, toilets, storerooms, workshops, a hospital and kitchens, a commandant's house and even a strong room for the soldiers' pay.

In the north, the Emperor Hadrian ordered a great wall to be built across northern Britain. It kept out war-like tribes that the Romans failed to conquer. The wall also helped the Romans to control trade between the north and the south.

Part of Hadrian's Wall. It was 117 km long (73 miles) and stretched from Newcastle in the east to Carlisle in the west.

Crack troops

The Roman Emperor had a professional army to help him conquer the enemy. Roman soldiers were fit, well-equipped and well-organised.

The army was divided into legions, each with about 5,000 men called legionaries. There were also 120 cavalry (troops mounted on horseback). Only Roman citizens could become legionaries. Other troops, called auxiliaries, were signed up from other parts of the Roman Empire. When an auxiliary had served in the army for 25 years he could become a Roman citizen.

Part of the Roman wall that once surrounded the fort at Chester, Cheshire. It kept attackers out and reminded the local people of the power of the Roman Empire.

There were three major forts in Britain: Chester, York and Caerleon. Smaller forts were built at other important places. Look out for the remains of a Roman fort. (Ask your local museum where to find the nearest.) Find out what you score on page 14.

Soldiers were trained to use weapons. They did fitness training including swimming and route marches, just like soldiers today. Soldiers also acted as military policemen, escorts for guard duty and clerks. Each legion had soldiers who were trained architects, engineers and surveyors, and craftsmen who made and repaired all the equipment.

8

Living like Romans

Life for many people in Britain changed enormously under Roman rule.

The Romans built towns with proper sewage systems, public bathhouses and toilets. Wealthy men and women lived in Roman-style villas such as at Lullingstone in Kent and Fishbourne in Sussex. The Romans encouraged trade with other countries and imported luxury goods from them. New-style fashions, entertainment, laws and government were brought in.

The Roman baths in Bath, Avon. The paving stones round the baths are Roman but the columns were built much later.

When you get home . . .

. . . make this real ROMAN CURE FOR DIZZINESS. You will need: a small glass bottle with a cork or stopper, vinegar and fresh mint. Pour some vinegar into the bottle until it is three-quarters full. Tear up the leaves of mint and put them in the vinegar. Put the cork or stopper in the bottle. Shake the mixture up and leave for 24 hours. Take out the mint and store the bottle of vinegar in a cool place. If someone feels a bit dizzy hold the bottle under their nose.

Lookout!

Look out for the remains of Roman towns and villas. At Wroxeter Roman City, Shropshire you can even see the gym where the townspeople worked out. Find out what you score on page 14.

Goodbye Romans

When the Romans had ruled in Britain for almost 400 years, the Roman Empire started to break up. The Roman Emperor decided he could no longer protect Britain from attackers and stopped sending money to pay the army.

Some Roman soldiers left Britain and went to fight elsewhere. Others stayed, married local girls and found other jobs. By 410, Roman rule in Britain had come to an end. People were left alone to face pirates who invaded from Northern Europe.

In troubled times, people often buried money and
other treasure. They usually planned to uncover it
when danger had passed. Archaeologists have
discovered hoards of hidden treasure in many
parts of the country.

Look out for
hoards of
Roman coins
in museums.
Find out what
you score on
page 14.

*This silver covered
dish is part of the
Mildenhall
Treasure from
Roman times. It
was found buried
in Suffolk. You can
see it in the British
Museum, London.*

No part of this publication may be reproduced by any means without prior permission of Newbery & England.

Text: Elizabeth Newbery

Design: Nicole Griffin

Main illustrations:
© Clinton Banbury

Other illustrations:
Sarah Beatty

Photographs:
© Jarrold Publishing

Production: Newbery & England

Publication in this form © Jarrold Publishing, Norwich 2000, latest reprint 2003

Concept & text:
Newbery & England 2000

3 North St, Osney Island, Oxford OX2 0AY

ISBN 1 84165 010 2

4/03

How to use the stickers

First find what you've got to look for under **Lookout!** Then peel off a sticker with the right number of points and stick it in the blank circle.

Score 15 for Celtic weapons

Score 10 for Roman weapons

Score 10 for a Roman road

Score 20 for a Roman fort

Score 15 for a Roman town

Score 15 for a Roman villa

Score 20 for a visit to Wroxeter

Score 20 for a hoard of Roman coins or treasure

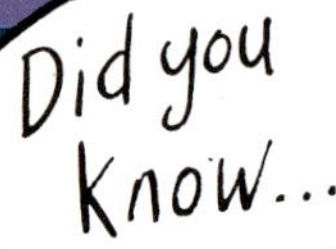

. . . that the Romans built the first public toilets in Britain? . . . that the Romans called anyone who wasn't part of their world a 'barbarian'? Inside you'll find more fantastic facts, STICKERS, jokes and how to make a real Roman CURE FOR DIZZINESS.

Lookout! guides to collect now:

- Castles
- Paintings
- Abbeys and Cathedrals
- Invaders

Why not put all your LOOKOUT! guides in a brilliant LOOKOUT! binder costing £5.00 (inc. p&p to UK address). Write to Jarrold Publishing, Healey House, Dene Road, Andover, Hants SP10 2AA. Sales 01264 409206; Enquiries 01264 409200; Fax 01264 334110 e-mail: heritagesales@jarrold-publishing.co.uk or visit our website: www.britguides.com

collect Lookout! guides

ISBN 1-84165-010-2

9 781841 650104